VALUE ADDED CUSTOMER SERVICE

EVERY EMPLOYEE'S GUIDE FOR CREATING SATISFIED CUSTOMERS

by
TOM REILLY

Published by

MOTIVATION PRESS

M P

St. Louis, MO

Library of Congress Cataloging-in-Publication Data

Reilly, Thomas P.

Value Added Customer Service: Every Employee's Guide
for Creating Satisfied Customers

Other Books by Tom Reilly:
Value Added Selling Techniques
Value Added Sales Management
Selling Smart

First Printing - 1995
Second Printing - 1995

Library of Congress Catalog Card Number: 94-079761
International Standard Book Number: 0-944448-10-0

Printed in the United States of America by Motivation Press.

Acknowledgments

I would like to acknowledge the following people who contributed to this project:

Charlotte Reilly, my wife, whose editing skills helped us produce a quality product.

Linda Huizenga and Jan Franklin who typed, edited, proofed, typed, edited, proofed, typed, edited proofed ad nauseam. Their diligence and commitment to this product made a significant difference in its outcome.

Jeff Herschel, our illustrator, whose creativity added another dimension to the book.

Dedication

I dedicate this book to you for the countless times you've gone the extra mile in serving your customers—especially when the only recognition you received was a feeling of self-satisfaction.

CONTENTS

THE
GUT-PUNCH QUESTIONS...

Are we right for each other?

GUT-PUNCH QUESTIONS

- *Am I better off being a prospect for your company or a customer of your company?*

- *Will you treat me better when you're courting my business or once the sale is consummated?*

- *After you have my business, will your attitude change?*

- *Once the honeymoon is over, how will I describe your service?*

AUTHOR'S NOTE: These questions are attention-getters! Now that I have your attention, please read on...

INTRODUCTION

Another book on customer service...just what the world needs! You can walk into any bookstore or library today and the business shelves are jam-packed with books on customer service. This is exactly what the world needs...more, and better, customer service. In fact, the world needs to hear this message a lot. Check into a hotel; order room service; go to a restaurant; take your automobile for repair; go to the post office, or sit in your doctor's waiting area for an hour, and you'll understand how desperately the world needs to hear this message over and over again. Customer service is a topic that screams for attention.

This is why I wrote *Value Added Customer Service*™: American business needs it. We need to raise the awareness level that service is an ongoing, all-the-time issue...not a sometimes issue. In bad times, companies scramble to offer better service to gain competitive advantage. In good times, they lose interest in offering the kind of service customers want and deserve. And yet, that's the best time to offer great service.

I've written this book to help everyone in the organization sing out of the same hymnal. Whenever I present a seminar on value added selling or value added sales management, seminar attendees ask, "What can we do to get our inside folks to practice the message we're preaching on the outside?" It's difficult for salespeople to brag about service to customers when they lack the confidence that inside people will deliver on these promises. It's equally frustrating for the inside people to know they're unable to deliver everything the sales force has promised. This is one of the obstacles to customer service—a breakdown in confidence and communications between the inside and outside folks.

So I've written this book to help salespeople communicate their message internally also. I did not write this book to create a market for customer service seminars, although that's the natural consequence of a book like this. Mostly, I've written this as a primer on building a value added service culture.

A value added service culture is one in which everyone in the organization *feels* and *acts* accountable for creating satisfied customers...

It begins with an attitude of service, and the behavior is free.

As an employee, you're either adding value or cost. And there's no job security in being a cost center to your organization. Your worth to the company increases proportionately to the value you add with your performance. High-performance, value-adding employees are gold for any organization.

So who's this book really for? It's for salespeople who have been through my Value Added Selling Techniques™ course and are looking for follow-up ideas to completely absorb the value added philosophy; it's for a management that's dedicated to creating a value added service culture, and it's for all levels of employees who really want to make a difference with their dedication and action.

This book is for the Human Resources Department to distribute to all employees for their use as a handbook on delivering value added customer service. This is for other speakers or trainers to purchase and distribute in their programs. It's for anyone who is passionate about raising the level of service in their organization. It's for you and everyone else in *your* organization.

I began this book with a few guiding principles: simplicity, practicality, and effectiveness. There's too much complex, high-level stuff on the shelf right now. Real customer service is more about serving. Customer service is not rocket science.

I began with a goal that this book must make gut-level sense to the average employee—not just management. Any person in the organization must be able to pick up this book and say, "I believe that. I identify with that. That makes a lot of sense to me," and then feel motivated to want to do it. The ideas in this book must be easy to implement—nothing complex—gut-level simplicity.

Finally, this book must make a difference in creating a culture of effectiveness for serving customers. Effective and efficient service is the yardstick of success. To quote one of my customers, "It's not good enough that the apple shines if the inside is rotten." I wrote this to help your organization shine inside and out.

In this book, I'm sharing a business philosophy that has developed over the past twenty years of business—thirteen of which I've spent as a speaker/trainer working with some of the best companies in the world: Milliken & Company, Harley-Davidson, Purina Mills, Anheuser-Busch,

Enterprise Leasing, Apple Computer, and the list goes on.

As the reader, you might ask, "What's in it for me?" Your investment in reading this short yet content-rich book will challenge some of your fundamental beliefs about serving customers. It will be a mind-stretching experience: a journey to inspire as well as to inform.

Good luck, and happy reading!

Tom Reilly

1

Peak Competitors

One advantage of my job as a professional speaker is working with some of the best corporations in the world. Over the past thirteen years, I've learned as much from them as they've learned from me. And one of the things these great organizations have taught me is how to compete.

There are two ways to compete. One competitor has an external competitive focus. They compete with other companies—to meet or beat them. They look for ways to be as good as or better than the competition. They either choose to equalize; that is, be as good as another company, or to differentiate—to be better than another organization. In either case, they use an external reference standard to measure success. "If we perform *as well as or better than* XYZ Company, we're on target!"

Another competitive style is the Peak Competitor. Peak Competitors have an internal competitive focus. They compete with themselves not others. Peak Competitors are value-adding, customer-serving organizations. They run toward something versus away from something. They're passionate about their potential. They challenge themselves with questions like, "How good are we?" and "What is our real potential?"

Because of this internal competitive focus, they're neither limited by their competitions' successes nor inhibited by their failures. They've discovered one of the universal truths of life...

When you compare yourself to other people, you either feel smug because you're so much better, or frustrated because you're not as good.

Peak Competitors share three common denominators. One, because they are internally competitive, they live by the question *"Is this the best we can do with the resources we have?"* If not, they reach a little further.

On an individual basis, employees who work for Peak Competitor organizations also challenge themselves with these questions: *"Did I bring my best me with me today?"* *"Did I bring my best presentation with me or did I leave something back at the office?"* *"Is this the best I can do, or can I do better for the customer?"*

Because of this internal competitive focus, they're unrestrained by yesterday's successes or failures. For them, life is an evolving, emerging process—always becoming more today of that which they're capable of becoming.

A second characteristic is that Peak Competitors believe in continuous growth and development. The Japanese popularized the notion of Kaizen: daily, continuous improvement of the product. Peak Competitors take this concept a step further to include the continuous growth and development of their people. They're passionate about potential and growth...

People are growing, evolving, emerging organisms—always becoming more of that which they're capable of becoming.

They're running toward something rather than running away from something. The neurotic fixates on perfection. Peak Competitors pursue excellence... *"We can become more of our potential."*

A third Peak Competitor characteristic is an unyielding optimism about the future. They believe their best day is on the horizon, not in their wake. They understand that their past is not their potential. Optimism fuels their engine. It provides them energy to continuously grow, develop, stretch, and challenge themselves.

The TQM movement has spawned an era of benchmarking. Companies use benchmarking to improve the quality of what they sell. On the one hand, benchmarking is a good idea because it says "Look what others have accomplished. We ought to be able to do the same."

On the other hand, benchmarking has the potential for becoming an artificial ceiling for many companies. If your competitive focus is external and you benchmark another organization, you may artificially limit yourself to their success. You may also be intimidated by their failures. When you benchmark another organization and your competitive focus is internal, you say, *"Look what they're able to accomplish. Sure it can be done, and I bet we can take it a step further."*

The Peak Competitor philosophy is the foundation for a value added service culture. Value added service is deeply rooted in the philosophy of maximum performance, not minimum standards.

This is a rock-solid foundation for your future: belief in your ability to grow. To be a Peak Competitor you must feel a productive discomfort with the status quo—a restless curiosity about your potential.

To create the value added service culture in your organization, you and others must live and work by the Peak Competitor philosophy. Challenge yourselves with the Peak Competitor questions...

"What's the most we can bring to the table?"
"How can we improve this today?"
"Is this the best we can do with the resources we have?"
"What next?"
"Where do we go and grow from here?"

Each begins with the premise and the promise that there's room for growth; there's room for development; there's always a better way.

2

Universal Rules Of Business

Value added service cultures follow the Universal Rules of Business. As you read, think about your company.

Rule #1: Everyone in your organization is a salesperson. Everyone in the organization sells something to someone. Bosses sell change to employees; employees sell new ideas to bosses; one employee sells a project to a fellow employee, and everyone sells to customers. Everybody in the organization sells something to someone. Do you buy this? Do you accept that you're a salesperson? Is this "sales spirit" part of your organization's business culture?

Rule #2: Not everybody believes Rule #1. Because of the negative bias many people hold toward salespeople, most folks do not perceive themselves as salespeople. Too many people have an "operations" mindset: "We're paid to push product through, not deal with customers." Or, they may have a bad case of *professionalitis:* "We're paid professionals (accountants, engineers, et al.). We don't sell anything to anyone. We allow them to buy." WRONG! Customers let you sell to them. Ironically, much of my business today comes from those who are not traditionally seen as salespeople. They've accepted Universal Rule number one.

Rule #3: Not everyone in the organization behaves like Rule #1. This is fairly self-explanatory.

Because you don't believe you're a salesperson, and you don't believe that most people in the organization are salespeople, you feel no need to behave like a salesperson. You do your job and the heck with the customer. In reality, everything you do affects the customer either directly or indirectly.

Rule #4: Everyone in the organization has a customer. There are the traditional customers: the users of your product, the people whose payments become your paychecks. We call these *external customers*. There are also *internal customers*. *Internal customers* are other employees in your organization whom you serve. For example, human resources serves everyone in the organization. Their *internal customers* are other employees. The credit department is the *internal customer* of the sales department. Data processing serves many other folks within the organization.

Employees are a boss's *internal customers*. Research and development serves the marketing department. Customer service is the *internal customer* of the sales force. The sales force is the *internal customer* for the product managers. Administrative assistants serve bosses. Other employees you serve are *internal customers*. They deserve the same great treatment you would normally give an external customer. They depend on you as much as the external customer depends on your organization.

Value Added Customer Service

Here are some facts about serving customers...

- *Anything and everything you do to serve your internal customer has an outward rippling effect on how well you serve your external customers.*
- *You can only serve your external customers to the degree that you serve your internal customers.*
- *Customer satisfaction mirrors employee satisfaction.*
- *Happy employees create happy customers.*

It's difficult to have satisfied customers without satisfied employees. Therefore, your behavior on the inside affects your performance on the outside.

Rule #5: Value added selling is not a spectator sport. Everyone in the organization is involved because it's a performance-oriented philosophy. In my selling seminars, the single greatest concern I hear is how well inside people will deliver what salespeople promise. Everyone in the organization is accountable for creating satisfied customers. It's not something that anyone in the organization can sit by idly and watch. It's something in which everyone must be actively involved. There are no spectators in this sport—only active, enthusiastic participants.

Rule #6: As a value added team member, your energy either adds to the team's momentum or it serves as drag on the team. This is another way of saying that you're either building it up or breaking it down—hurting or helping. Every employee is either a profit center or a cost center to the organization. When you consider this, it's a challenging thought...

"Am I building this company up or breaking it down?"
"Am I a cost center or a profit center?"

Remember, there's no security when your performance costs the organization money. Your security and future are directly related to how much value (not cost) you add.

When you look at the energy you bring to the job, is it a constructive, building kind of an energy, or is it a negative, destructive type of an energy? Organizations need positive energy to grow and compete.

Rule #7: "We is greater than me." This is the natural outgrowth of the belief that everyone is accountable for creating satisfied customers; that value added selling is not a spectator sport, and since everyone serves each other, the synergy of everyone's working together creates a momentum greater than the sum of the individual parts.

I was speaking at a national sales meeting a number of years ago when the director of operations raised his hand and asked, "Tom, please clarify something for me. When we say the customer purchases from us, is it the salesperson's customer, or the inside staff's customer, or is it **our** customer?" Obviously, he had an agenda to promote. The rift in his company between inside and outside was great. This inspired me to write an article **Whose Customer? Our Customer!** You see, it's not the sales force's customer, but **everyone's** customer in the organization.

For salespeople reading this, you must accept that. Why? Because if you promote an atmosphere of "my customer" in the organization, other employees feel no need to take care of "your" customer. On the other hand, if you promote "our" customer, you'll get the performance you desire for the customer. "*We* is greater than *me*" is everyone in the organization moving toward a common goal of serving the external customer either directly or indirectly by serving their internal customers.

The philosophy of serving customers begins with a fundamental competitive philosophy of challenging yourself to find out how good you really are and an acceptance that everyone in the organization is accountable for serving the customer. As you continue reading this book, you will see this philosophy surface over and over again: a philosophy of challenging oneself, personal accountability, and service to others.

Rule #8: Value is three things. First it's whatever the customer says it is: it's **personal**. Customers, not sellers, define value. Second, value is **perceptual**. Perceived value is the gift wrap on the package—the promise that builds anticipation. And, it's the customer's perception of value that ultimately counts. Your performance affects the perceived value of your service. Your tone of voice, attitude of helpfulness, professional image, knowledge, and initiative shape perceptions of value.

If perceived value makes customers feel good about buying, **performance** value makes them feel good about owning and using what you sell them.

Performance value is the profit impact you make on the customer's business or life.

Peak Competitor, value-adding, customer-serving organizations define value in customer terms, offer tons of perceived value, and deliver more performance value than the customer expects.

Rule #9: Everyone must belong to something. One of our most fundamental yet dominant needs is the sense of belonging. Our earliest life experiences focus on the socialization process—to get in step with society. Everyone needs to feel they belong somewhere. That's why we have country clubs, motorcycle gangs, professional associations, fitness centers, support groups for anything and everything, etc. Everyone wants and needs to belong somewhere.

This also applies to your customers and fellow employees. Do they feel like they're part of your organization? Do you make them feel like a vital member of your group? Do they enjoy this sense of belonging or do they feel isolated or alienated? For every customer and employee you fail to engage, embrace, or bring into the fold, there's another organization out there that would love an opportunity to make them feel welcomed and important. They would love for your employee or customer to feel a strong sense of identity with their group.

Your prescription is simple: embrace them; make them feel a part of something, and genuinely welcome them into your organizational family.

As you review this list of Universal Rules of Business, how many of these are relevant to your organization? How would you answer these questions...

- *Does everyone in our organization view themselves as salespeople?*

- *Does everyone behave as a salesperson?*

- *Do your employees serve other employees (internal customers) with the same dignity and initiative they serve external customers?*

- *Is everyone in your organization an enthusiastic and positive influence in the process of serving?*

- *Whose notion of value are you selling?*

- *Do your employees make the customer feel like they belong?*

3

You The Customer

I'd like for you to think about a recent situation in which you were the customer and received less than what you would call full-quality service or treatment. Think about it for a few moments...what was the one thing the person did or said that really frustrated you, and what could they have done differently to salvage your feelings?

When I ask this question in my Value Added Customer Service training sessions, I typically hear the car dealer scenario in which a female seminar attendee describes how she was condescended to because she was a woman. I've heard grocery store scenarios: spoiled produce, incorrect change, or failure to honor coupons. Post offices and license bureaus always top the bad service list. The stories go on and on. We never run short of examples.

In all cases, the seminar attendees say what really frustrated them was the people with whom they dealt. They treated them like an interruption or an intrusion. For example, I recently searched for a new laser printer for our office. I went to one of the national chain computer superstores and approached two clerks who were standing at a computer screen playing a video game. I stood there for a couple of minutes until one of them happened to notice. He asked, "You need something?" and I said "Yes. I'd like some information on a laser printer."

He said, "Hang on a minute," and finished what he was doing with the video game. "Okay, what do you need?"

I explained what I was looking for and he said, "Well, let's look at some products." I asked about the difference between a $1,500 printer and a $5,000 printer. He responded, "Well, one's obviously more expensive than the other."

When I asked if he could be a little more technical for me he got this disgusted look on his face and said, "All right, let's look at the product sheets." As he looked at the sheets he said, "One's got some different stuff on the inside than the other. Do you want anymore information?"

I said, "No, thank you," and left without the printer. As I left, the irony blew me away. This company brags about the level of service they offer, yet I was treated as an intrusion and interruption. This company spends hundreds of thousands of dollars annually to promote a service advantage, and his behavior took the "super" out of superstore and the "value" out of value added reseller.

Be clear on something from the start...

You're not doing the customer a favor by serving them. They're doing you a favor by giving you the opportunity to serve them.

Let me repeat that so everyone reading this is 100% crystal clear on this concept. The fact that you are serving a customer is your privilege, not the customer's privilege for your serving him. The customer should not thank you...you should thank him. If you have trouble with that, find another job. You're in the wrong position. *If you have no desire to serve others, get out of your current position and find a job in which you do not interact with anyone.*

The list of frustrations I hear goes on and on: condescending treatment, no authority to make decisions, poor product knowledge, bad information, slow service or no service. There's nothing new about this treatment. It's as old as the hills.

There is a simple yet fundamental law of human nature that's relevant to customer service. I call this the first great reality of customer service...

The same things that frustrate and alienate you as a customer are the very same things that frustrate and alienate your customers.

And it's never the big things. It's always the little stuff that irritates us: someone misspells our name; they frown at us when we walk in; if they're doing something else, they treat us like an interruption. It's always the little things that aggravate us—it's rarely the big stuff.

It's also the small things that irritate your customers: being put on hold for an extended period of time; misspelling names on invoices and letters; shipping the wrong materials; shipping to the wrong address; printing invoices with incorrect pricing; failure to return phone calls, or not being properly acknowledged. These are not major issues on the surface, but they have major consequences for us with the customer. Again, the small things that really aggravate you are the same things that aggravate your customers.

Value Added Customer Service

Another interesting exercise is to consider a scenario in which you were treated well. Make it one that you could actually brag about the service you received. What happened? What impressed you? Again, when I ask this question in seminars, I hear the flip side of the first exercise. "I went to a car dealer and they took the extra step of providing me with a free loaner." "I walked into an electronics store and the sales clerk greeted me, thanked me for being there, and projected an air of helpfulness without shoving product down my throat." It's the supplier whose customer service rep called to proactively inform you of a backorder situation. It's someone at the license bureau who read some flexibility into the regulations and gave you the benefit of the doubt rather than hiding behind the bureaucracy. It's the empowered employee who made a decision on her own in favor of the customer.

A second customer service reality is...

The same things that impress you and cause you to return to do more business with a company are the same things that will impress and encourage your customer's return.

And just like the negative things, it's always the small things that make a difference: smiling at a customer; using their name often; thanking them; not leaving someone on hold too long; offering assistance; correcting things before they become problems. These are examples of how empowered employees proact to deliver better service and create satisfied customers. This is how companies gain competitive advantage with their people. Is your performance on the job creating more of these positive or negative scenarios? If I were to interview your customers, which would they convey to me?

4

What Is Customer Satisfaction?

When I ask this in seminars, I hear a variety of things: customer satisfaction is when your customers return with their friends; customer satisfaction is when the customer thanks you for providing service; customer satisfaction is when the customer orders more, or customer satisfaction is when customers tell their friends.

All of these are correct in a sense. They're examples of customer satisfaction. Customer satisfaction is defined as a ratio: it's the relationship between your performance and the customer's expectations. If you out-perform their expectations (i.e., exceed their expectations) you have satisfied customers. If you under-perform their expectations, you have dissatisfied customers. A simple formula to use is...

Customer satisfaction is a function of your performance relative to the customer's expectations.

If you promise a lot and deliver more, you'll always create satisfied customers.

For salespeople, this means promise only that which you know you can deliver. For inside folks,

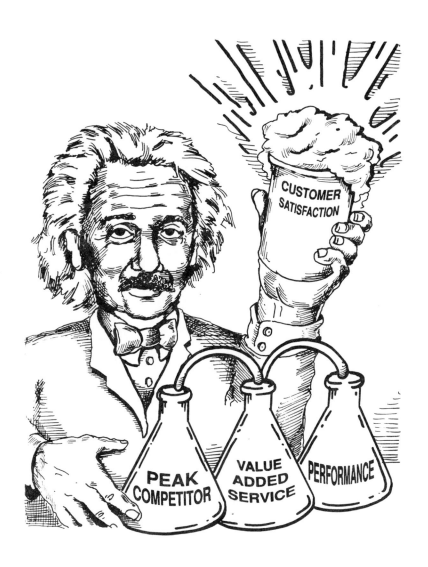

deliver everything promised. The prescription for management is when performing a customer satisfaction survey, make sure that the variables you measure are your performance relative to the customers' expectations. It's a simple way to gauge what your customers are feeling and thinking. And remember that it's the customers' perceptions that ultimately count. Your view of your service is interesting but irrelevant to serving customers. It's how they feel that really counts.

5

What Is Customer Service?

When I ask for a definition of customer service in seminars people respond with, "The customer has a problem and we fix it," or "The customer has a question and we answer it," or "There's an issue and we take care of it." It reminds me of walking into one of the large national discount stores and seeing a desk off to the side with a sign hanging above it, CUSTOMER SERVICE. The implication is that if there's a problem that's where you go to fix it.

In each of these definitions, *reacting* is the key. In other words, unless there's a problem, you don't get service. Unless you have a question, you don't get an answer. Unless there's an issue, you don't get attention. These are examples of serving the customer. But, customer service is more than that...

Customer service is a philosophy in which all employees feel and act accountable for creating satisfied customers.

Look at the key words in that definition: all employees. Value added selling is not a spectator sport. Everyone sells something to someone. Accountability is vital to customer service, and everyone is accountable. *There's never a "that's-not-my-job" mentality when it comes to serving customers. It's always your job to serve customers.*

Value Added Customer Service

Another key word is *creating* customer satisfaction. It's something you must do actively. Everyone in the organization is responsible for and works to exceed the customer's expectations.

In too many organizations, customer service is a department, a group of people, or a section in the store where someone goes with a problem or complaint. Customer service *must* be an attitude within your organization. It must be fundamental to your business philosophy, not a department. Too many companies, too many managers, and too many employees pay lip service to customer service. Customer service must be a fire in your belly—a passion to serve customers. It's a commitment to ensure that customers leave more excited than when they walked in the door. It's also your insurance policy for future business.

Imagine a family saving money for months to purchase a new television set. They've cut corners, denied themselves, and set aside their discretionary income. They've read the consumer reports; they know which model they like; they're excited, and the anticipation is overwhelming. They've planned this event for weeks. They visit your store, and you provide them with the type of service that most customers only dream about. You're friendly and knowledgeable; you understand all the different models currently on the market; you understand the customer's needs and are able to match them up with a product that absolutely satisfies their needs, and you give them the type of service they will brag about to their friends. Imagine how purchasing that television is a peak experience for the family. It's a continuation of the excitement and anticipation they've felt for weeks and months of saving for this. That's the way business is supposed to happen.

Wouldn't you like to be treated that way when you're the customer?

Now, contrast that with a scenario in which the customer has the same burning anticipation yet meets an employee who doesn't care, doesn't know much about the product, and has more of a "let's-get-it-over-with" mentality. It deflates the customer. They had tremendous anticipation but were let down by the seller. It's easy to imagine yourself in that situation. Your customers are in that situation every day and deserve better.

Serving customers is a unique opportunity for employees. Few jobs in any organization carry the impact of an employee's creating satisfied customers. Your treatment of the customer is more powerful than all of the advertising dollars in the budget...

Advertising draws the customer to your organization initially. Your performance brings them back or chases them away.

Serving customers well is also the gracious thing to do. Treating them with grace and class makes the customer feel great while giving you the instant gratification of a job well-done.

6

Why Provide Value Added Service?

Simply, it's the right thing to do. Customers have expectations, and your responsibility is to exceed those expectations: give them everything they're looking for and then some! From the customers' perspective, it's the right way to treat them. From your perspective, it makes tremendous financial sense. On average it costs 5-6 times more to get a new customer than to keep an existing one happy. Organizations that reduce their customer attrition rate (the business they lose out the back door) by 2% experience the same savings as an across-the-board 10% cost-cutting campaign.

The White House Office on Consumer Affairs asked this question, *"Why do people stop doing business with a company?"* Over two-thirds said they quit because the seller didn't care enough to keep their business: they were indifferent.

Organizations that use service as a competitive advantage are able to charge more for their goods and services, get it, and outgrow the competition in market share. It makes incredible financial sense for organizations to develop the service mentality. The more service you offer, the less important price becomes in the decision. Value-adding, customer-serving companies have discovered that when it comes to serving customers...

There's no traffic jam on the extra mile!

Proactive, value-added customer service enables companies to sell more profitably and compete more fiercely in the marketplace. Responding to customers' problems and issues in a way that satisfies customers is one of the cheapest forms of advertising. The average customer who has a problem tells nine or ten people about it, and 13% of those people are going to tell twenty or more people. Customers who have complained to an organization and had their complaint resolved satisfactorily tell an average of five people about the wonderful service they received.

Since companies are composed of people, and people are imperfect, you must accept that mistakes happen—it's human nature. The key is containment. This means that your goal must be to contain the errors, mistakes, and defects within your organization as much as possible. The road to perfection is the journey of the neurotic.

On the other hand, the pursuit of excellence is a noble endeavor. People make mistakes. Your focus must be the containment of these mistakes within your company walls. Some might argue that if you're having brain surgery, perfection is better than containment. I agree. But most of us aren't practicing brain surgery. The pursuit of excellence supported by a philosophy of continuous improvement encourages people to give their best every time. For the manager who demands perfection, I would ask, *"Are you the perfect boss?"*

Containment of mistakes is not a cop-out. It's not permission to get sloppy. It's true acceptance that these things happen. Containment protects your customer while preserving your reputation.

If your goal in serving customers is to satisfy their needs *and then some*, you're living the pursuit of excellence. The *and then some* habit is a simple philosophy that says, "We'll take care of the customers' needs...*and then some*. We'll handle the customers' concerns...*and then some*. We'll go the extra mile...*and then some*." It's the *and then some* philosophy that creates the customer satisfaction you want.

So, when you ask that question, "Why should we deliver better service?" the answer is because it makes sense financially. Second, it's the right thing to do. It's the way customers deserve to be treated. And third, it makes sense for you as an employee.

I spent seven years of my life studying psychology. The one thing of which I'm absolutely convinced is that people want to do a better job today than they did yesterday, and a better job tomorrow than they do today. I have a very positive view of workers. I believe the majority of people want to feel that they're contributing; what they do is meaningful, and what they do makes a difference in this world.

Each of you wants to be better today than yesterday, and better tomorrow than today. Developing the value-added, serving attitude is an opportunity to do that. It's the quality of workmanship, the pride of workmanship, and the feeling of serving that makes going to work everyday worthwhile. It's your contribution to this world.

7

Why Don't Companies Deliver Better Customer Service?

There are four reasons why companies don't deliver better customer service. All four of these are really erroneous assumptions. **First, "It requires too much time to deliver better customer service."** They see themselves as being too busy to deliver customer service. They feel it requires too much time on their part to serve their customers better. Ironically, it requires more effort to get a new customer than to keep an existing one happy.

Second, "It's too expensive to serve the customer." It costs more to get a new customer than to keep an existing one happy. What does it really cost, in terms of time or money, to thank a customer? What is the real cost of, when putting a customer on hold, returning within one minute to see how they're doing? What is the real cost of doing the job right the first time? On the other hand, quality gurus estimate that 35% of the cost of something has to do with quality problems. Some companies believe that it requires too much effort and concern, and companies don't feel they can make that investment. Can they afford not to?

Third, "We're fine the way we are." "We're cool." "We believe we're doing a great job." These organizations really believe everything's peachy. The boss may set this tone and everyone falls in

lockstep thinking. They just don't know how the customers perceive them. Perhaps they've never taken the time or made the effort to ask the customer, *"How are we doing?"* Remember, it's always the customer's perception that counts.

Fourth, "We-don't-care." If you've ever been on the receiving end of this arrogance, you understand how malignant it really is. Maybe they have too much business now, and because things are so good they feel they don't have to care. In reality, this attitude sets the stage for future business. If your company has the *attitude of ingratitude*, polish your résumé. You'll need it. Customers tire of this mindset.

Whether it's ignorance, denial, or arrogance, each is a prescription for failure. If you see these attitudes in your company, there's an urgency to act now.

8

Danger Signals

There are early-warning danger signals that indicate you're not delivering value added customer service. Customers give plenty of warning about your service: the customer calls less than before; you've noticed an increase in customer complaints about delivery, quality, service, or price.

Another warning signal is the *Freudian Slip*. The customer calls you and uses a competitor's catalog number. You see a competitor's coffee mug in their office or a piece of competitive literature on their desk. All signal that the customer is shopping around.

There are internal signals also. Internal signals are things you notice within your organization. You begin to believe you're invincible, "We're the best, therefore, people need us more than we need them." Another internal signal is when you have a *pain* versus a *gain* mentality. You begin looking at the customer as more of a pain to your business than a gain to your business. You view them as an interruption or intrusion rather than a welcomed opportunity.

A third internal signal is the *transaction mentality*. This is where you narrowly focus on just getting the job done. Your concern for process, procedure, and guidelines overrules your good sense for serving the customer. Expediency and speed versus service become your goals. Employees

with transaction mentalities often find themselves saying things like, "We can't do it that way because of company policy." A transaction mentality is the employee who is more concerned about getting the order filled than filling a need for the customer.

The following quiz is a customer service test I developed for a company to determine the level of service they're offering:

1. Do you view the customers' questions and visits as interruptions?
2. Are you difficult for customers to contact?
3. Do you routinely ask the customers "How are we performing for you?"
4. Do your employees, peers, and management like your customers?
5. Do you feel it's too costly to serve customers?
6. Do you thank every customer for his or her business?
7. Have you ever said "We're the only game in town. We don't need to serve"?
8. Is it important to serve customers in good times as well as bad times?
9. Will you open a closed store or office to help a customer?
10. Do you get all the repeat business you should?
11. Have you said "If they would just leave me alone I know I could get my job done"?
12. Is customer satisfaction a guiding principle in your business?

For each "yes" response on questions 3, 4, 6, 8, 9, 10, and 12 give yourself one point. For each "no" response on 1, 2, 5, 7, and 11 give yourself one point. If you scored from ten to twelve points, your company offers great customer service. If you scored from seven to nine points, you need help. If you scored six or less, you're in deep trouble.

Customer service is not rocket science. Customer service is giving the type of treatment you hope a family member would receive when dealing with a seller.

These danger signals can serve as your own internal barometer to determine how desperately your company needs help in this area. Your motivation to change will start the process. Your dedication will keep it on course.

9

Win With Value Added Customer Service

In this section we'll explore strategies for winning with value added customer service. These ideas are easy-to-implement, common-sense thoughts. They can be performed by everyone in your organization. The first few ideas concentrate on your attitude. The second group of ideas deals with behavior.

DEVELOP THE ATTITUDE OF GRATITUDE

Everything in life begins with an attitude, a thought, or an idea...

Developing the attitude of gratitude means living your passion for service. It's walking your talk.

The attitude of gratitude is the gut-level passion employees feel about serving the customer. Thackeray said *"...life is a lot like a mirror. You get back what you put into it."* I call this the boomerang effect in life: what goes around comes around. Contrast this with a concept I introduced earlier in the book, the "attitude of ingratitude": the obvious and malignant lack of concern or appreciation for the customer's business.

If the desire to serve is in place, the behavior is free. Employees who feel a passion for service automatically find ways to deliver better service to the customer.

I was presenting a customer service program one day to a group of distributors when one of the participants raised his hand and asked, "Are you suggesting that we be nice to all of our customers?"

My response was, "No, just the ones you want to keep." He nodded in agreement and said, "That makes sense."

I looked at him thinking "He still doesn't get it." It all begins with attitude.

Whatever people feel on the inside, they generally show on the outside. If you feel that the customer is an interruption, aggravation or intrusion into your day, you will unwittingly, unconsciously, or nonverbally communicate that feeling to the customer. On the other hand, if you begin with the attitude that the customer is a valuable asset to your business—vital to your future—you will find ways to validate that.

To create a value-added, customer-serving organization, you must focus on the attitude you bring to the table. *If you want to serve the customer, you will find ways to make it happen.* Desire drives action. If you respect and appreciate your customer, your behavior reflects it.

STRETCH YOUR TIME HORIZON

One reason employees fail to deliver great service is that they have a transaction mentality. They only focus on getting the job done as quickly as possible; they view the interaction with the customer as a necessary evil for processing the order. They're more interested in filling an order than serving a customer. This defines commerce too narrowly.

Stretching your time horizon means realizing that your interaction with the customer is but a moment along a time continuum—a grain of sand in an hourglass. There will be many more moments, or grains of sand, in the future depending on how well you treat the customer.

Stretching your time horizon is understanding and accepting that how you treat customers today determines your future opportunities to serve. Even small orders today are potential big orders tomorrow. It could be your customers' way of testing you. Happy customers return with their friends.

One of the least understood and under-utilized business principles is *leverage*. Leverage is your getting a greater return for the same amount of effort. It's repeat business from customers. It's customers selling you to their friends. It's cross-selling additional products for greater account penetration. Most businesses fail to fully leverage their existing base of customers.

When you stretch your time horizon, you accept that the business you do with customers has a much longer time line than the moment of transaction. It includes repeat and referral business. This attitude is mandatory for great service.

BE PROACTIVE

Proactive is a word used extensively in the human resources field. It means anticipating and taking the initiative, being a self-starter, not waiting for something to happen, nipping it in the bud. Compare this to *reactive* which means waiting for something to happen. When you're proactive, you anticipate and act. This is vital to customer service because many crisis issues you deal with can be avoided by developing a more proactive mindset.

A proactive, value-added, customer-serving mindset is taking the initiative to resolve issues before they become problems. It demonstrates concern for the customer and avoids more serious consequences of a problem growing out of control.

An example of proactive, value-added customer service is the company that handles my cellular phone. A couple of years ago, someone from their organization called me and said, "Mr. Reilly, I've been studying your phone bill, and it appears to me that you're not on the right plan considering your usage habits. In fact, if you were on a different plan you could have saved $75.00 last month on your cellular bill. Would you like me to switch your basic usage plan?" Naturally, I agreed.

Her proactively dealing with this situation meant that I was less inclined to respond to advertised specials by the competition. She also promoted a tremendous amount of goodwill by volunteering to save money for me. This is proactive, value-added customer service...

Proactive, value-added customer service means never having to say you're sorry to the customer.

When you're proactive, you look for ways to serve the customer before problems become problems. This is a first cousin to the old saying "An ounce of prevention is worth a pound of cure." *You anticipate and act.*

Look at your job and organization. What are some ways in which you can become more proactive in serving the customer? Is it studying invoices for mistakes? Proacting to backorders to find alternative solutions? Offering alternatives or options for shipping problems? Anticipating customer demand and calling with information prior to allocation situations? Any of these demonstrate your concern and initiative for serving the customer. You can live by this simple formula...

Anticipation plus Action equals Proactive, Value-Added Customer Service

---

43

PERCEIVING IS BELIEVING

This is a variation of the old philosophy that the customer may not always be right, but the customer is always the customer. Perception is subjective reality. What I see is reality for me. Since perception is colored by one's needs, wants, and desires, what I see may be completely different from what you see. In business, it's the customer's perception that always counts. Your perception is interesting to you but irrelevant to the customer.

There are scenarios in which you know you're right and feel the need to argue that point with the customer. Are you more interested in winning over the customer or winning the argument? There are countless thousands of situations when the seller has won the argument, but lost the customer. Which is more important to your long-term success?

My perception as a customer of your service counts more toward my satisfaction than your perception of your service. Your focus must be on what the customer believes. Customer satisfaction involves two key elements: your performance and the customer's expectations. Your performance is judged by the customer's perceptions, and it's those perceptions that drive customer satisfaction.

Customers have their own way of seeing things. The only way to ensure you're offering great service is to play to the customers' perceptions and not yours...

Great service only becomes great service when the customer says it's great.

Your opinion of your service compared to the customers' opinion of your service is a growth opportunity—a gap to be filled—a great place to start.

IT'S EASIER TO ASK FORGIVENESS THAN PERMISSION

This is another way of saying *"Take action; make a decision; do something."* One of your customer's greatest frustrations is dealing with powerless, low-initiative, no-risk employees. For employees reading this book, *"Asking forgiveness is easier than asking permission"* means serving your customer well and dealing with it on the spot. Then go back to management and say, "I offered this alternative to the customer as a way to serve them better."

For the managers reading this book, it's vital that you empower your employees with guidelines so that they can make a decision on the spot to serve the customer. How many times have you asked to speak to a supervisor to get results?

Employees who feel they have some power to make decisions are more committed to serving the customer.

Those who feel powerless are reactive: "I can't do anything." They communicate that attitude to customers which adds to the frustration of the situation. I've seen numerous occasions in business in which employees have taken the initiative to solve a problem for the customer and management totally supported them realizing that their goal was not to destroy the organization but to build it by serving the customer.

Live on the edge a little. Take a risk. Make a decision. Suggest alternatives. Be creative. And remind your boss that your intention is a noble one: customer satisfaction.

LIVE THE PHILOSOPHY: *PROMISE A LOT AND DELIVER MORE.*

Exceed customer expectations. Employees who live this philosophy focus on creating realistic customer expectations and on delivering more than the customer expects. If you exceed their expectations, you've got happy customers. If you under-perform their expectations, you have dissatisfied customers. Living this philosophy, *"Promise a lot but deliver more,"* is what I referred to earlier in the book as the *"and then some"* philosophy. It reminds me of a candy store I visited.

I selected from several barrels of assorted candies and took them up to the cash register. The clerk rang them up and told me the cost. He then reached in a barrel, grabbed a handful of candy to throw in. He gave me some candy ("and then some"). Now I'm smart enough to realize that this was built into the price of what I bought, but it was still nice to get a "freebie."

When I lived in New Orleans, the Cajuns had their own term for this. They referred to it as Lagniappe: a little something extra that was unexpected. It always makes people feel good.

Value Added Customer Service

"And then some" applies to more than throwing in extra product. It's not just free goods. It applies to effort also. It's giving extra attention to detail and extra initiative to the customer. When the customer sees that you believe in serving them...*"and then some"*...they realize that your performance exceeds their expectations. That's customer satisfaction.

Work on developing this attitude. Look for ways to apply it in your job. Even the small things make a difference. Go the extra mile... *"and then some!"* Do more than what's expected. Be an extra miler! Make it a habit to go out of your way to serve.

Promise a lot and deliver more.

THE CUSTOMER'S BILL OF RIGHTS

Every customer has fundamental rights he can expect the seller to meet. This is the Customer's Bill of Rights. In my customer service programs, I ask a question of the group and then give them 15 or 20 minutes in a small group discussion to complete this exercise. The question is, *"What six things do your customers have a right to expect when they purchase something from your company?"* I hear amazing responses like "Our customers have a right to expect...

- Quality products with great service at a competitive price;
- Available inventory;
- Knowledgeable salespeople with no hassles;
- Courteous and respectful treatment;
- To be treated as the most important thing in our day;
- Accuracy in quoting and billing."

(Signed, the employees of XYZ Corporation.)

What amazes me most when I ask this question is their spontaneous consensus on the customers' fundamental rights. Everyone knows, at a gut level, what customers deserve. When you review the above Bill of Rights, its brilliance is its simplicity. This is not a list management constructed in a strategic planning session and jammed down the employees' throats. It's a set of beliefs that employees hold and are committed to. It's a simple yet powerful exercise. This list should be highly visible, celebrated, and spotlighted within the organization. Put it on the back of a business card;

make a one-page flyer to include in a literature kit, or print posters to hang throughout the office.

Everyone in the organization must contribute to the Customer's Bill of Rights. Because of their participation and input, employees feel accountable for delivering value added customer service.

IDENTIFY OBSTACLES TO VALUE ADDED CUSTOMER SERVICE

Everyone in the organization can easily answer this question. *"What are some of the things that get in our way of delivering better customer service?"* Employees answer in certain ways; management answers in other ways. How do your systems contribute to or detract from serving customers? Are they cumbersome? Are they antiquated? Do they no longer make sense?

How do the people in your organization contribute to or detract from serving the customer better? Do you have "people obstacles"? Because of their attitudes, are your employees roadblocks to better customer service? Because of a lack of initiative, do they perceive artificial boundaries?

These are great discussion questions to identify the problem areas and the remedies. For the managers reading this, go straight to the source. Ask your employees for their opinions. They're closer to the waste or inefficiency. They may see it more readily than you. Look for obstacles in your organization...they're there.

NAIVE LISTENING

I'm unsure who first coined the expression, *naive listening*. When I consider *naive listening*, I think of how children listen to stories: mouths hung open, eyes clearly focused on the storyteller, and their whole being absorbed by what they hear. Children listen to stories, hear the subtleties, and feel the message. That's how you must listen to customers.

It means listening to absorb everything: verbal and nonverbal. It's non-defensive listening. You're not listening for blame, you're listening for problems and concerns. It's listening as a child might listen.

Sometimes people just need to blow off steam. A willing ear and interested heart can make a real difference. Naive listening is the ability to diffuse a situation by hearing another's concerns and empathizing. Research proves that companies that listen to customers' concerns have a greater probability of customers not only coming back, but bringing friends with them.

Naive listeners reflect what customers say: they feel, they understand, and they repeat it to clarify their understanding. The customer sees and appreciates this. It would be wonderful if, at the end of an interaction, the customer were to walk away and say, "I didn't realize I had so much to say. I guess it had a lot to do with the fact that the other person just wouldn't stop listening."

FIX THE PROBLEM NOT THE BLAME

Do you think that the customer really cares about whose fault it is or how it happened? Absolutely not. He couldn't care less. The customer is not interested in fixing the blame, he wants to fix the problem. Too many people are willing to pass the blame on to someone else for whatever reason. Perhaps it makes them feel more secure in their position or they want the customer to know they wouldn't be stupid enough to make this kind of mistake. In reality, the customer doesn't want a lengthy explanation on who's to blame for a situation. All he wants is a solution.

Blame is a useless concept. Blame spends a whole lot of time with negative energy and finger pointing. Accountability is important to remedy the situation so that it doesn't happen again. Blaming is such a waste of time when other people really want resolution. If your focus is, "Who can I pass this off on," you're spending too much time covering your backside and not enough time covering the customer's needs.

The moral is...

Don't get defensive...get busy.

"MACH ONE" RESPONSE TIME

Mach One is the speed of sound. Mach One response time means responding to the customer as quickly as possible. Why? You want to avoid the situation getting worse. Buyers react more positively to quick resolution than with slow resolution. Slow response allows their frustration to simmer and burn. It never gets easier when you wait to deal with a bad situation. Seek ways to reduce your response time. Handle the customer's problem immediately and you can advance to more positive issues with your customer.

This relates to the strategy of identifying customer service obstacles and fixing the problem, not the blame. Listen naively to what the customer says, and respond quickly. Don't get defensive.

Mach One response time also means assessing your systems and finding ways to make it easier for your customer to get information. Mach One response time is not restricted to crisis management. It can be a proactive approach to make it easier for your customer to do business with you. Expedite your ordering system. Reduce the time it takes for you to process orders. Use time as a competitive weapon. Make it your friend, not your foe.

FOLLOW-UP!

This is the number one weakness for salespeople: i.e., the lack of follow-up they deliver for the customer. I've always given salespeople the benefit of the doubt in believing that they have wonderful intentions but; somehow, the follow-up just never seems to happen. It's not intentional neglect; however, their good intentions never seem to materialize.

You can improve customer service by delivering what you promise—making good on your commitments. Follow-up is not limited to salespeople. This applies to any employee in the organization. Anytime someone makes a promise to the customer, she must follow up.

Follow-up is also important when you're proacting to customers' needs. When you see a potential problem situation and you proact to it, you must follow up to ensure corrective action is taken.

Following up to thank the customer is another important aspect of customer service. It's calling the customer back after she's placed an order to ask how the solution is working for her. Follow-up is the sale-after-the-sale. Follow-up is delivering the promise. Follow-up distinguishes you from the competition. It's a simple, easy-to-implement concept. *Follow-up is promising what you'll do and then doing what you promise.*

Do-It-Right-The-First-Time

There's an old saying, *"If you don't have time to do it right, when are you going to have time to do it again?"* This sounds more like a time management principle—and indeed it is. Yet, this also applies to quality issues. Quality pundits estimate that 35% of the cost of something is attributable to mistakes: doing it wrong the first time. Phil Crosby, an expert in quality, wrote the book <u>Quality Is Free</u>. He says "...it's not quality that costs money, it's the unquality things...quality is really free, it's the mistakes that cost."

Whether you're in a hurry, you're handed a last-minute assignment, or the customer pushes for results, the motivation doesn't matter. What matters is if you don't do it right the first time, it complicates the situation and makes dealing with it the second time even more problematic. Begin with realistic expectations of what you can accomplish and give the needed effort to ensure the work is right for the customer the first time.

These questions will help...

"Is this the best we can do?"
"What next?"
"Where do we go from here?"

Slow down and do the job right the first time. Focus on the results that will make the customer happy. Remember, it's the customer's perceptions that count not yours. Do more than what you've promised and you'll keep the customer satisfied. It all hinges on your doing it right the first time, every time. Will you make mistakes? Sure. Mistakes happen. But, the idea is to contain the mistakes within your area so that the customer doesn't have to experience them. People make mistakes. It's understandable to make mistakes. The pursuit of excellence is a whole lot different than the pursuit of perfection.

Pursue excellence in what you do and contain mistakes so the customers don't have to experience them.

Attention to detail is the difference between "okay" service and great service. Make and take the time to do it right the first time. Managing the details plus focusing on the end result add up to great service.

CROSS-SELL

Cross-selling is a hybrid of selling and serving. It's where you help your customer by suggesting other products, services, or divisions within your organization that can help him. When you cross-sell, you also help your company by lowering the cost of doing business in addition to the extra sales revenue.

Customers appreciate it because they have already established credit with your company; they've built a relationship based on trust, and it saves them time in searching for other sellers. This also helps cement the relationship with your customer. The more levels at which you connect, the stronger the ties.

Look for ways to cross-sell other products and services your organization provides. Offer referrals to other people in your company who can make a difference. Look for the natural ways in which products and services connect. For example, computers need printers which need ribbons, toner, and periodic maintenance. Capital equipment needs replacement parts and service. Banking customers can use checking accounts, savings and money market accounts, safe deposit boxes, CDs, trust services, etc.

If you're not cross-selling your full line of products and services, you're missing a great opportunity for your organization. More importantly, you're not giving the customer the full range of benefits that come with your total value added solution. For every customer you serve, ask yourself the cross-sell opportunity question...

Which other products and services would benefit my customer?

SERVE INTERNALLY

Internal customer service is just as important as external customer service. Internal customers are those people within your organization whom you serve. External customers are the traditional types. Remember, everything you do to serve your internal customers has an outward rippling effect on your external customers. And, you can only serve your external customers to the degree that you serve your internal customers.

Internal customer service breaks down in those organizations where political in-fighting and sibling rivalry are commonplace. With all the competition your company has on the outside, you don't need to add to it by creating a culture of conflict. Armies that battle within their ranks don't win wars. *Serve internally to serve better externally.*

"How do I serve my internal customers?" First of all, determine who they are. Second, what do they need from you? Build a service delivery system that handles those needs...*and then some!* Everything we discussed about how to deliver better external customer service can be applied to these internal customers also. Remember, employee satisfaction is a mirror of customer satisfaction. Anything you do that contributes to employee satisfaction (internal customer service) contributes to customer satisfaction.

PERSONAL ACTION PLAN

This wrap-up activity I do in my customer service programs makes the message relevant for everyone in the seminar. This is a personal action plan. The first question I ask is, *"What are some front-line, customer-serving activities you can do in your job to improve customer satisfaction?"* I hear responses like: thanking the customer every time for his business; smiling more often at the customer; greeting the customer with enthusiasm to let him know that he's a valuable asset; never leaving the customer on hold for more than 30 seconds; always asking if customer complaints can be relayed to management so that management knows what's happening; offering a little bit of extra to satisfy the customer when he's dissatisfied; listening in a non-defensive way to customer concerns, etc. Seminar attendees list half-a-dozen front-line ideas for better service. If everybody in the audience did half of what they said they would do, customer satisfaction would skyrocket!

The next question I ask is, *"What are some things you can do behind-the-scenes to improve customer satisfaction?"* What's different about behind-the-scenes efforts is that you'll rarely get credit. Nobody knows you're doing it. This is truly a case of when the satisfaction of doing the job well must be enough. These are not high-visibility actions. These things avoid problems. For example, you anticipate a backorder situation and do something internally to take care of the customer. The customer may never see a problem because of your action. It's creating a solution before the problem becomes an issue. One example is presenting management with an issue before it becomes a major aggravation for a customer. Another example is your double-checking an invoice for accuracy. The customer gets exactly what she expects, and you get the satisfaction of knowing you did everything within your power to create a satisfied customer. Going the extra mile and doing it right the first time, every time, are examples of behind-the-scenes activities.

This is a useful exercise for everybody reading this book. Ask and answer the question...

"What are a half-a-dozen things I can do, both face-to-face with the customer and behind the scenes, to improve customer satisfaction?"

In this section, we've presented a number of ideas for delivering better service to create satisfied customers. *Serving your customer begins with an attitude of gratitude: a passion to serve.* If you don't want to serve people, you're in the wrong business or the wrong job. **If you want to serve people, the behavior is free.** You'll automatically react and proact in ways that create satisfied customers.

Serving your customer is as simple as treating others (both inside and outside your organization) in a way that you would hope your family is treated—with respect and an eagerness to please.

Value Added Customer Service

In an era of complexity, customer service is a breath of fresh air. It's a return to the core values of business: service, respect, value, integrity, and concern for the welfare of others. Incorporating these values into your everyday business practice guarantees the top-drawer treatment you want your customers to receive. And, you sleep better at night knowing that those whom you serve get the best treatment available anywhere.

*Lead your people and
manage the process.*

10

Thoughts For Management

In this section, I want to offer some suggestions for managers on creating greater customer satisfaction and an attitude of serving within your organization.

Cultures change top-down, bottom-up. Cultures change slowly over time. Change is a process, not an event. Cultures, like people, evolve and emerge from wherever they are currently to wherever you want them to be. To create the value-added customer serving culture...

You need to understand that you must lead your people and manage the process.

Be consistent in what you say and do. It must be a case of, "Do as I do, *and* do as I say." Employees model your behavior as they listen to your words. If you're talking from both sides of your face, employees notice. If you're saying things one way yet behaving another, they follow your behavior not your words.

There's a peak competitor movement afoot that emphasizes daily, continuous improvement of people not just product. Investing in your product, systems, technology, research, and quality process are necessary investments in your business and your future. You must invest in your employees

too. Invest in their continuous improvement and development. Empower them. Give them the authority and autonomy needed to make a decision so they can respond and proact to customers' needs, offer solutions, and feel accountable in their jobs.

Remember, customer satisfaction mirrors employee satisfaction. If you have problems with customers feeling dissatisfied, you probably have dissatisfied employees. Your employees are your internal customers. I realize this is a difficult concept for many people to accept.

The way you treat your employees is the way they treat your customers.

The tone of your culture is the product of your own efforts. Your attitude determines the employees' attitudes. It's difficult for employees to respect customers when they hear management complain about *"those damned customers."*

I was at an auto dealership recently whose owner I know well. He despises 95% of his customers. Can you imagine how that 95% are treated? Employees in his organization say things like, *"This guy can take his business somewhere else. We don't need him."* You know the treatment these customers receive. The word on the street about this dealership is not very flattering.

What if your employees had a customer satisfaction budget? A customer satisfaction budget is a *10% slack factor.* Do your employees have the freedom to cut the customer some slack? Will you allow them *10% grace* to create satisfied customers? When you consider the cost of getting a new customer versus keeping an existing customer happy, is a 10% error in the customer's favor *(i.e., cutting the customer 10% slack)* really that big of a deal?

This is not a campaign of automatically giving the customer 10% on everything. It's when employees feel like they have some latitude in offering the customer solutions that will make them happy.

What if your bonuses were tied to customer satisfaction? What if you initiated a program within your organization in which profit sharing and year-end bonuses were tied to customer satisfaction not gross revenue? At the end of the year, survey your customers and compare their satisfaction with last year. If it compares favorably, offer your employees an opportunity to share in the satisfaction they've created. If there's less satisfaction, you have a goal for the following year.

11

Thoughts For Salespeople

You'll recall the story I told earlier in this book about a director of operations asking me the question, "Tom, I'm confused about something and perhaps you can clear this up. I know oftentimes we hear our salespeople talk about 'our' customer and people on the inside talking about 'my' customer. Whose customer is it anyway? Is it their customer or is it our customer?"

Certainly he had an agenda or an ax to grind. He was disgusted that salespeople feel so protective of customers that they don't inspire teamwork. He also felt irritated that inside folks may not feel like it's their customer. Everyone in the organization must feel that it is **our** customer. It's not **your** customer as a sales rep, it's not **my** customer as an inside person, it's **our** customer.

If you communicate to everybody within the organization that this is **our** customer, they feel more committed to serving **our** customer. You benefit directly but, more importantly, the customer benefits from this philosophy. And ultimately, that's why you're in business—to serve the customer.

As a salesperson you can increase customer satisfaction if you do a better job of communicating with people on the inside. Communicate what you've promised the customer. Let people on the inside know of specific problem situations. Let management know about service problems you've witnessed within your organization. Often, customer satisfaction issues boil down to simple communication or the lack of it.

Another way you can build customer satisfaction is don't over-promise. Certainly you can promise a lot if you can always deliver more than that which you promise. Inside folks complain that salespeople over-promise. Make sure that your promises are reasonable for your organization. And be sure that your team members on the inside know what you've promised.

Give credit and recognition to inside people who deserve it. If you aspire to be a manager, one of the things you must be willing to do is let your employees take credit for the good work they've done. This is part of leadership. It's also good human relations.

You might as well begin building some of those skills right now. Give credit, recognition, and celebrate your successes with your team members. Be willing to share the fruits of your efforts as well. Celebrate it with letters of recognition. Send high-visibility recognition letters that everyone in the organization can appreciate. Realize that the people on the inside are your team. It's not "us" in the field against "them" on the inside. It's you and your inside people working with your customer's team to solve a customer's problem. It's your working for the customer with your inside team. If you view yourself competing with the inside for the customer's goodwill, then you've got huge problems. You and the inside people are working as a team to satisfy the customer's needs. Imagine the improvement in customer satisfaction when a team of people are working toward this goal.

12

Final Thoughts

I wrote this book to address an issue that all companies live with...customer satisfaction and improving customer service. I began with a simple premise. This book is more about philosophy and ideas than technique. It's written to cause you to think about customer service from a gut-level perspective. Customer service must be an attitude within the organization for any organization to survive and thrive. Customer service is not rocket science; it's not brain surgery. It begins with an attitude and (when the attitude of serving is in-place) the behavior is free.

For those reading this who want to make a difference in their organization, begin by reviewing how you look at the customer. Is your customer valuable to your organization? Are they vital to your successful future? If the answer is yes, then you must develop a passion for satisfying the customer—to exceed his expectations. Once you develop the attitude of serving, the behavior is truly free. You will naturally act in those ways which increase customer satisfaction.

Good luck, and happy serving!

Tom Reilly

Personal Action Plan™

Based on your reading of this book, please list six things you plan to do to deliver better customer service—internal and external. Be specific and realistic. Share this list with your manager.

1. _____

2. _____

3. _____

4. _____

5. _____

6. _____

This is my pledge to deliver better customer service to create more satisfied customers. In my way, I'm making a difference in our organization.

_____   _____
Signature   **Date**

SALES MOTIVATIONAL SERVICES
©1995

70

Other Products by Tom Reilly

Books

- Value Added Customer Service™ $ 5.00
- Selling Smart™ $ 9.95
- Value Added Selling Techniques™ $19.95
- Value Added Sales Management™ $24.95

Cassettes

- Value Added Selling Techniques™ $49.99
  (4-cassette album)
- Communicative Selling Skills™ $59.99
  (6-cassette album)
- Relationship Selling™ $25.00
  (2-cassette album)

Courses and Speaking Topics

- Value Added Sales Management™
- Value Added Selling Techniques™
- There's No Traffic Jam on the Extra Mile!™
- Time and Territory Management
- Relationship Skills™
- Value Added Customer Service™
- Proactive Selling Techniques™

For Additional Information Contact:

Tom Reilly, President
Sales Motivational Services, Inc.
171 Chesterfield Industrial Boulevard
Chesterfield, Missouri 63005
314-537-3360